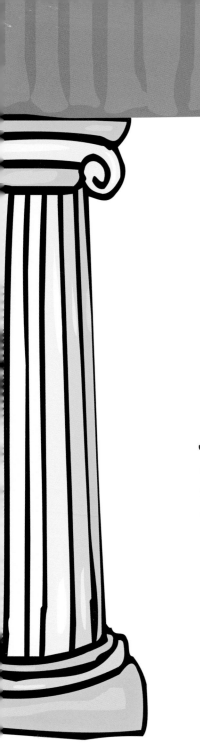
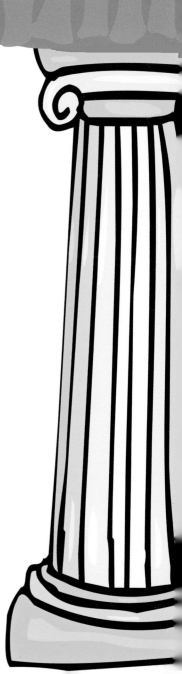

CHARACTER COUNTS

CARING COUNTS

by Marie Bender

Reviewed by
Dr. Howard Kirschenbaum, Ed.D.

ABDO
Publishing Company

visit us at
www.abdopub.com

Published by ABDO Publishing Company, 4940 Viking Drive, Edina, Minnesota 55435. Copyright © 2003 by Abdo Consulting Group, Inc. International copyrights reserved in all countries. No part of this book may be reproduced in any form without written permission from the publisher.

Printed in the United States.

Photo credits: BananaStock Ltd., Brand X Pictures, Comstock, Corbis Images, PhotoDisc, Skjold Photography

Editors: Kate A. Conley, Stephanie Hedlund

Design and production: Mighty Media

Library of Congress Cataloging-in-Publication Data

Bender, Marie, 1968-
    Caring counts / Marie Bender.
      p. cm. -- (Character counts)
    Summary: Identifies the personality trait of caring and discusses its importance and ways in which it can be practiced at home, in school, with friends, and in the community.
    Includes bibliographical references (p.) and index.
    ISBN 1-57765-869-8
    1. Caring--Juvenile literature. [1. Caring.] I. Title.

BJ1475 .B46 2002
177'.7--dc21

2002066692

Internationally known educator and author Howard Kirschenbaum has worked with schools, non-profit organizations, governmental agencies, and private businesses around the world to develop school/family/community relations and values education programs for more than 30 years. He has written more than 20 books about character education, including a high school curriculum. Dr. Kirschenbaum is currently the Frontier Professor of School, Family, and Community Relations at the University of Rochester and teaches classes in counseling and human development.

CONTENTS

CHARACTER COUNTS

Our character is what we do when we think no one is looking.

—H. Jackson Brown, Jr., author

Your character is the combination of **traits** that makes you an individual. It's not your physical traits, such as the color of your eyes or how tall you are. Rather, character is your thoughts, feelings, beliefs, and values.

Your character shows in the way you interact with your family, friends, teachers, and other community members. People who are well liked and successful are said to have a good character. Many traits build good character. Some of these traits include caring, fairness, honesty, good citizenship, responsibility, and respect.

Good Citizenship

Responsibility

Respect

Honesty

Fairness

Caring

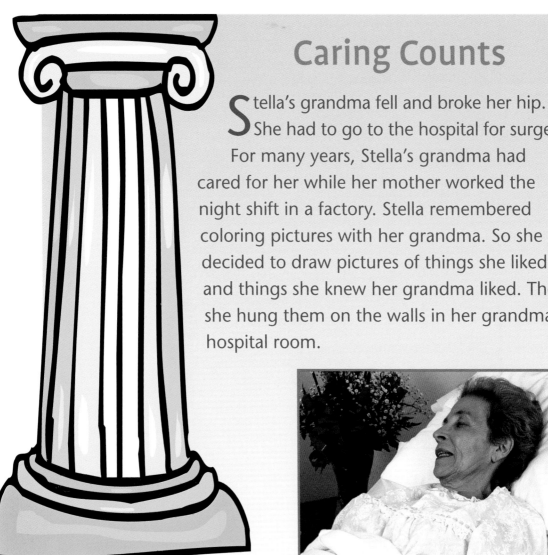

Caring Counts

Stella's grandma fell and broke her hip. She had to go to the hospital for surgery. For many years, Stella's grandma had cared for her while her mother worked the night shift in a factory. Stella remembered coloring pictures with her grandma. So she decided to draw pictures of things she liked and things she knew her grandma liked. Then she hung them on the walls in her grandma's hospital room.

Stella visited her grandma every day. They talked about what happened at school and at home. Stella also played cards with her grandma and told her jokes to cheer her up. She said that she hoped her grandma would get better soon so she could come home.

Stella made caring count.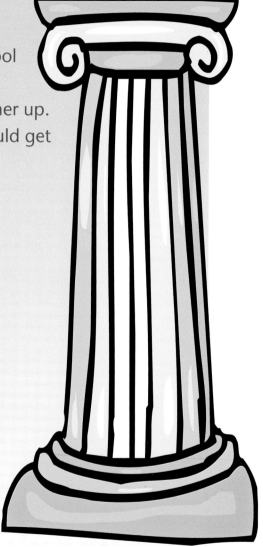

WHAT IS CARING?

Love thy neighbor as thyself.

—The Bible, Leviticus 18:19 and Matthew 19:19

Caring is being concerned about other people and what happens to them. Those who place other people's feelings and needs before their own are caring. Caring people try not to do or say things that

hurt other people's feelings. They also try their best to be respectful, kind, and to make others happy.

Many values are part of being a caring person. Kindness, generosity, thoughtfulness, helpfulness, and compassion are all values that show you care. You can **demonstrate** these values in different ways. For example, you can listen when others are talking to show you care about what they think and feel. You can also share

your possessions and time to show you are generous and unselfish. If you help people in any way, you show you are willing to reach out to others.

Caring is not expecting something in return for being kind. If you think you deserve a reward for being kind, you may be disappointed if you don't receive one. Caring people don't do kind things so others will do something for them. But when you show people you care about them, you attract others who truly care about you and treat you kindly in return.

Have you ever wondered what would happen if no one cared about anyone or anything? Without caring, nobody would have any friends, and families would not be close. **Charities** would not help poor or sick people, and the environment would be in danger. The world would be a sad, lonely, cruel, and unhealthy place to live without caring people.

Luckily, the world is full of caring people, and you can see it every day. Whenever people help someone else, smile at a stranger, spend time with family, share things with others, or recycle **aluminum** cans, they show that they care. Caring is contagious. That means when people show they care by doing good deeds, others will want to do the same.

Think about it...

How do you feel when someone treats you unkindly?

What does it teach you about how you should treat others?

Nobel Peace Prize Winners: People Who Cared

When people care, they can change the world. The Nobel Peace Prize recognizes people who have made efforts to promote peace. Some of the winners are listed below.

Year: 2001
Winners: The United Nations and its secretary general, Kofi Annan of Ghana
Accomplishment: Working for a better organized and more peaceful world

Year: 2000
Winner: President Kim Dae Jung of South Korea
Accomplishment: Working for democracy and human rights in South Korea and peace with North Korea

Year: 1998
Winners: John Hume of the United Kingdom and David Trimble of the United Kingdom
Accomplishment: Working for peace in Northern Ireland

Year: 1997
Winners: The International Campaign to Ban Landmines and its coordinator Jody Williams of the United States
Accomplishment: Working to ban and clear land mines

Year: 1993
Winners: Nelson Mandela of South Africa and Frederik Willem de Klerk of South Africa
Accomplishment: Working to peacefully end apartheid and establish democracy in South Africa

Year: 1989
Winner: The Fourteenth Dalai Lama (Tenzin Gyatso) of Tibet
Accomplishment: Working to improve human rights, environmental problems, and international conflicts

Year: 1979
Winner: Mother Teresa of India
Accomplishment: Helping suffering people

Year: 1964
Winner: Martin Luther King, Jr., of the United States
Accomplishment: Working on the American Civil Rights movement

Year: 1906
Winner: President Theodore Roosevelt of the United States
Accomplishment: Ending the war between Japan and Russia

CARING AND FAMILY

It is in the love of one's family only that heartfelt happiness is known. —Thomas Jefferson, third president of the United States

Your family members are the people that you care about the most. Showing them you care is important.

You can show your **siblings** you care about them in many ways. For example, you can help your little brother with his homework to show you care about how he does in school. If you walk to school with your sister, you can hold her hand when crossing the street to show you care that she is safe. You can tell your big brother a joke you heard to show you care about being his friend.

It is also important to show your parents you care. You can watch your baby brother while your parents are fixing dinner to show you care about sharing responsibilities. You can do your chores to show your mom you care about following her rules. Bringing your dad a glass of juice when he is sick shows that you care about helping him feel better. You can also talk to your parents about what you did at school or at your friend's house. They want to know what you do when you are not with them because they care about you, too.

Your parents show they care about you by setting rules that keep you safe and help you learn. You may not understand why your parents want you to go to sleep at a specific time every night. But it shows they care that you have the proper rest to do your best in school. You may think your parents are overly protective when they make you wear a helmet when you ride your bike. It shows they care, because they want you to be safe and respect the law.

Caring for your family also means helping around the house. You can keep your room clean and put away your toys. You can also help with chores, such as washing dishes, sweeping floors, emptying the trash, and raking leaves. This shows that you care about your family by sharing household responsibilities.

Ways You Can Show
Your Family You Care

 Take your dog for a walk.

 Play with your younger sibling.

 Help when you are asked to.

 Listen to others.

 Tell people that you care about them.

 Spend time with older people in your family, such as aunts, uncles, and grandparents.

 Write letters to or draw pictures for relatives who live far away.

Your relatives know you care about them when you invite them to be a part of your life. You can invite them to athletic activities, recitals, or special days such as birthdays and holidays. Some of your relatives may live far away. You can show them you care by sending letters, cards, pictures, or emails. You can also call them to find out how they are doing. Keeping in contact with your relatives shows you care about them.

CARING AND FRIENDS

The only way to have a friend is to be one.

—Ralph Waldo Emerson, American poet and essayist

You can show your friends you care about them in many ways. You can spend time together doing activities you both enjoy. Sharing your toys, inviting your friends to your house, and complimenting them when they do well in school or sports shows you care.

You can also ask your friends how they are feeling. If your friends are feeling sad, you can give them a hug and try to make them feel better. If your friends have problems, you can listen to them and try to help. You can tell your friends that you like them and are glad that they are your friends.

Part of caring for your friends is taking care of their things. If your friend lends you a book or game, you take care not to lose or damage it. You can show you care by returning it when you are

How do you feel when someone treats you unkindly?

What does it teach you about how you should treat others?

done. You can take care of things you borrow as if they were your own.
When you go to a friend's house, you can try not to make a mess. If you do,
you can clean up after yourself.

CARING AND SCHOOL

Be kind and merciful. Let no one ever come to you without leaving better and happier.

—Mother Teresa

Caring at school shows that you respect authority, classmates, and property. It means following the rules and paying attention to your teachers and the other adults in the school. You can be helpful by taking care of school property. You can also be friendly and courteous to your classmates.

You can show your classmates you care in many ways. You can lend them pencils when they forget theirs. Or, if classmates are having trouble with homework, you can spend time helping them. You can **congratulate** the student who won a prize at the science fair. Being friendly also shows you are a caring person. You can introduce yourself to the new person in your class and ask him or her to sit with you at lunch. You can organize a game during recess and let everyone who wants to play join in. You can help people who trip and fall and ask if they are okay.

Think about it...

How can you help your teachers or classmates at school?

You can show your teacher you care by paying attention in class. You can raise your hand to ask questions when you don't understand. After class, you can ask if there is anything you can do to help, such as erase the blackboard or put away books.

CARING AND COMMUNITY

Without a sense of caring, there can be no sense of community.
                                    —Anthony J. D'Angelo, author

Caring for your community means following the laws. It means being friendly to your neighbors. It also means taking care of the environment.

You can follow laws to show you care about others as well as yourself. For instance, you can wear a helmet when you ride your bike or skateboard to show you care about safety. You can cross a street at an **intersection** when the traffic light says "walk" to show you care about obeying the law.

There are many ways to be a caring person in your community. You can give clothes that you don't wear to a **charity**. You can volunteer to spend time with an older person in a nursing home. If you see litter on the sidewalk, you can pick it up and put it in the trash. You can join community organizations for children, such as the Boy Scouts, Girl Scouts, or the YMCA.

Think about it…

What can you do to show you care about your community?

To help care for the environment, you can **recycle** paper, cans, and bottles. You can help your parents plant a garden. If you catch a frog or turtle, you can let it go without hurting it. You can show you care for animals by not purposely scaring or throwing things at them.

CARING FOR YOURSELF

Friendship with oneself is all-important, because without it one cannot be friends with anyone else.

—Eleanor Roosevelt, first lady and American stateswoman

Don't forget to take care of yourself! Sometimes it is easy to spend so much time caring about others that you don't do things that make you happy.

You can care about yourself by taking care of your body and mind. To take care of your body, you can exercise, eat healthily, bathe or shower regularly, brush your teeth, and get enough sleep. To take care of your mind, you can do your best in school, and spend a little time each day doing activities you enjoy. You can read your favorite book, play a computer game, ride your bike, shoot baskets in the driveway, or talk to a friend. If you care for yourself, you will find it easier to care for others.

> Think about it...

What are some of your favorite things to do for yourself?

A Random Act of Kindness

No act of kindness, no matter how small, is ever wasted.

—*Aesop's Fables*

A **random** act of kindness is a great way to show caring. It is a little thing you can do to help someone or make someone feel good. It can be something you say, such as a compliment or wishing someone a good day. Or, it can be something you do. For example, you could help a classmate with an assignment or a **sibling** with an after-school chore. You could even teach a friend a new game.

A random act of kindness can also be a gift you give, for no reason except you want to make someone happy. The gift doesn't have to cost a lot of money. You can draw a picture for someone, give away your dessert at lunch, or pick someone a flower.

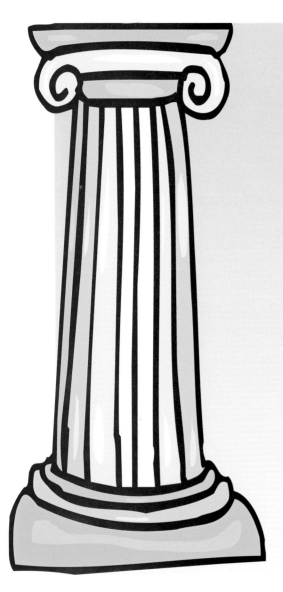

Twenty Random Acts of Kindness

 Eat lunch with someone new.

 Visit a sick friend or relative.

 Clean a neighbor's sidewalk.

 Give a friend or family member a hug.

 Make a new friend.

 Pick up litter.

 Call a relative who lives out of town.

 Open a door for someone.

 Help carry something for someone.

Cheer up a friend.

 Thank a teacher.

 Play a game with your little brother or sister.

 Offer someone your seat if the bus is crowded.

 Give your allowance to a charity.

 Read to a younger child.

 Let someone else go first.

 Give someone a compliment.

 Baby-sit for free.

 Give someone your dessert.

 Do something extra to help around the house.

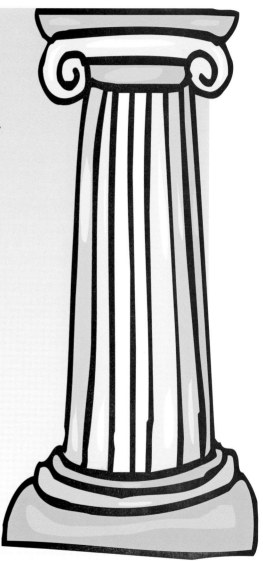

Sometimes a **random** act of kindness is something you can do for people you don't even know. For instance, if you're on your way to school and pass a house with some litter in the yard, you can pick up the litter and throw it away. A random act of kindness makes you feel good about yourself, even if no one knows that it was you who did the good deed.

Random acts of kindness show you are a genuinely caring person. By showing you care about your family, friends, teachers, classmates, and neighbors, you show that you care about yourself. You are building good character. In return, others will treat you kindly, proving that character counts.

Think about it...

What is a random act of kindness you have done but didn't even realize you were doing? How do you feel when you help someone without being asked? How do you feel when someone does something for you without you asking for anything?

CARING

Glossary

aluminum - a light, soft, silvery-white metal.

charity - an organization that gives help to the poor or needy.

congratulate - to express happiness or pleasure at the success or good fortune of someone else.

demonstrate - to make a show of; express openly.

intersection - the place where two or more roads cross.

random - unplanned or happening by chance.

recycle - to make suitable for reuse.

sibling - a brother or sister.

trait - a quality that distinguishes one person or group from another.

Web Sites

Would you like to learn more about character? Please visit www.abdopub.com to find up-to-date Web site links about caring, fairness, honesty, good citizenship, responsibility, and respect. These links are routinely monitored and updated to provide the most current information available.

INDEX

For the Character Counts series, ABDO Publishing Company researched leading character education resources and references in an effort to present accurate information about developing good character and why doing so is important. While the title of the series is Character Counts, these books do not represent the Character Counts organization or its mission. ABDO Publishing Company recognizes and thanks the numerous organizations that provide information and support for building good character in school, at home, and in the community.